Piano Concerto No. 1

in D Minor, Op. 15

JOHANNES BRAHMS

DOVER PUBLICATIONS, INC.
Mineola, New York

Bibliographical Note

This Dover edition, first published in 2004, is reprinted from Volume 6 *(Konzerte für Klavier und Orchester)* of *Johannes Brahms: Sämtliche Werke; Ausgabe der Gesellschaft der Musikfreunde in Wien*, originally published by Breitkopf & Härtel, Leipzig, n.d.

International Standard Book Number: 0-486-43910-0

Manufactured in the United States of America
Dover Publications, Inc., 31 East 2nd Street, Mineola, N.Y. 11501

Piano Concerto No. 1
in D Minor, Op. 15

(composed 1854–58; published 1861)

INSTRUMENTATION

2 Flutes [Flöten, Fl.]
2 Oboes [Oboen, Ob.]
2 Clarinets in B♭ ("B"), A [Klarinetten, Klar.]
2 Bassoons [Fagotte, Fag.]

4 Horns in D, B♭ ("B")-basso [Hörner, Hr.]
2 Trumpets in D [Trompeten, Trpt.]

Timpani [Pauken, Pk.]

Piano solo [Klavier]

Violins 1, 2 [Violine, Viol.]
Violas [Bratsche, Br.]
Cellos [Violoncell, Vcl.]
Basses [Kontrabaß, K.-B.]

Piano Concerto No. 1 in D Minor, Op. 15

9

14

PIANO

Rondo
Allegro non troppo

68